Pc

HONOLULU'S "ROYAL MILE"

Hotel Street from Alapai to Aala

GARY R. COOVER

Rollston Press

Pocket Walking Tour of Honolulu's "Royal Mile"
by Gary R. Coover

ISBN-13: 978-1-953208-19-4

Front cover: Royal Coat of Arms (King Kalākaua)

Portions excerpted from:

Honolulu Chinatown: 200 Years of Red Lanterns and Red Lights (Rollston Press, 2022)

Downtown *Honolulu's Lost Buildings & Forgotten Architects* (Rollston Press, 2023)

Pocket Walking Tour of Honolulu's Chinatown (Rollston Press, 2023)

Pocket Walking Tour of Old Downtown Honolulu (Rollston Press, 2023)

ROLLSTON PRESS
1717 Ala Wai Blvd #1703
Honolulu, HI 96815
www.rollstonpress.com

TOUR ROUTE

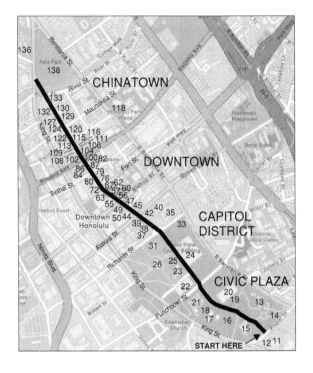

Buildings are identified by page numbers.

The tour begins at Alapai Street between the Frank F. Fasi Municipal Building and Municipal Parking Lot, and ends at Aala Park in Chinatown.

Table of Contents

A WORD ABOUT HAWAIIAN DIRECTIONS:

The cardinal directions of north, south, east, and west do not make much sense in an island setting, so these are the directions commonly used in Hawaii, and specifically in Honolulu:

Mauka (MAU-ka) = toward the mountains

Makai (ma-KAI) = toward the ocean

Ewa (EV-uh) = toward Ewa Beach

Waikiki (WAI-kee-kee) = toward Waikiki (1800's and early 1900's)

Diamond Head (or DH) = toward Diamond Head (in current use)

INTRODUCTION

Hotel Street runs through the heart of Honolulu, between Beretania Street and King Street, and goes through these four major areas:

- Civic Center Plaza
- Capitol District & Iolani Palace
- Downtown
- Chinatown

Hotel Street was one of the first streets in Honolulu, named after the Warren Hotel built sometime in the 1820's by Major William R. Warren.

The street initially ran from Maunakea Street to Richards Street through Chinatown and downtown.

After the 1886 Chinatown fire it was extended to River Street, and in 1902 the existing Palace Walk and portions of Printers Lane were widened and incorporated into Hotel Street, taking it all the way to Alapai Street.

For the creation of the new State Capitol and the City Civic Center, Hotel Street was once again closed off to vehicular traffic between Richards and Alapai streets.

Hotel Street c.1880, looking ewa from Smith Street

Hotel Street has long been a major ewa/waikiki thoroughfare in downtown Honolulu.

There was a Honolulu Rapid Transit streetcar line down the entire length of Hotel Street from 1901 to 1941, starting from the main Alapai Car Barn at the mauka/waikiki corner of Hotel and Alapai, and extending as far as King and Middle streets.

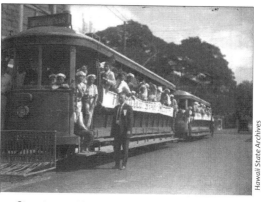

Streetcar at Masonic Temple on Hotel Street.

One of the biggest changes to Hotel Street came in the 1970's after a bus study in 1978 concluded that Hotel Street could carry up to 95-100 buses per hour.

At the time there were 1,800 buses on Hotel Street in a 21-hour day, carrying an estimated 50,000 passengers.

Long term plans called for potentially routing high-speed crosstown mass transit through Hotel Street.

In 1979, sidewalks were widened, and bus stops and routes were color-coded and identified with symbols: a red Hibiscus, blue surfer, green coconut palm, yellow pineapple, and brown tiki.

An $8M project designed by Parsons Brinckerhoff Quade & Douglass in 1987 established bus service both directions with 14' travel lanes, excluded all cars, and called for sidewalks between 9' and 13' wide between King Street and Richards Street.

Wheelchair ramps were added along with new street signs in English and Chinese.

Opening day was April 26, 1988. Hotel Street is still a bus-only transit mall 36 years later.

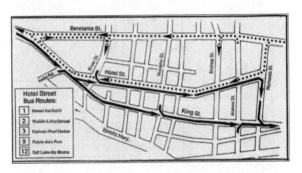

Hotel Street has been through many changes, and this flat, easily walkable tour will take you through its 200-year history while pointing out important buildings past and present, notable public art, plus stories of events which have shaped Hawaii's and Honolulu's history.

IOLANI PALACE IS THE ONLY ROYAL PALACE
IN THE UNITED STATES.

HOTEL STREET FROM AALA PARK TO
ALAPAI STREET IS EXACTLY
ONE MILE IN LENGTH.

THAT MAKES THIS IS THE ONLY ROYAL MILE
IN THE UNITED STATES!

Alapai Transit Center and Joint Traffic Management Center

2017

The Alapai Transit Center, Joint Traffic Management Center and accompanying 5-story parking garage cost $100M and was finally completed in 2017. StudioAxis from Indianapolis designed the JTMC.

In 1871 this was the site of Fernhurst, the home of Juliette and Joseph B. Atherton, so named because the grounds were covered in ferns and palm trees.

Julia Morgan designed a beautiful YWCA home for single working women that was built here in 1921. It was demolished for a trolley bus storage area in 1951. Bowling City (24 lanes) was built here in 1955, and converted into a bus barn in 1977.

The Honolulu Rapid Transit streetcar barn and power plant were located immediately mauka, where the Police Station and landscaped parking garage sits today.

"Hōkū Pa'a"

IMMOVABLE STAR

2020

S. Kazu Kauinana, artist

*"The figure is seeking navigational guidance from
Hōkū Pa'a – a constant beacon for wayfinders."*

ℌonolulu ℭivic ℭenter ℙarking ℨtructure

1979

Not many parking garages are considered artistic or extraordinary, but Takashi Anbe's design for the $7M Honolulu Civic Center Parking Structure deftly conceals the parking for 939 cars by covering it with a bermed roof garden 5 to 14 feet above street level along with three huge circular openings for fresh air and large monkeypod trees.

Curved pathways wind through the park, which includes the Seagull School's Early Education Center for children 18 months to 5-years-old that opened in 1986.

"This magnificent open space, a carefully designed and maintained park, offering the most unexpected view of Honolulu's civic and financial districts…. That this prosaic, obviously utilitarian and barren structure was converted into such an inspired place of beauty can only be called a miracle." – Alfred Preis

"TUBERS"

1998

Jodi Endicott, artist

Look mauka and look up just past the entrance to the parking garage and you'll see three whimsical characters surfing the large grassy wave that hides the parking garage and overlooks Alapai Street.

A graduate of the University of Hawaii in Manoa, Jodi Endicott is a local artist and environmental advocate living in Kailua.

Her works have been shown at the Tokyo Metropolitan Art Museum, Hawaii State Art Museum, Maui Arts & Cultural Center, Hui No'eau in Makawao, as well in in Korea and Khatmandu.

This installation is one of many throughout the Frank F. Fasi Civic Center, all part of the City of Honolulu's public art program.

FRANK FASI BUILDING

1975

Originally called the Municipal Office Building, this towering structure was designed by Wiliam Svensson of Naramore Bain Brady and Johanson, architects.

The design was selected from 43 entries, with a $8M budget for the 2.2-acre site. The jury selected Svensson's design, calling it "powerful, direct and beautiful…the building recognizes the visual relationship between its location and the Capitol."

"It stands directly and simply on the ground, allowing open space to flow through it and pass around it."

One critic called the style "Penitentiary Modern".

In 2006 it was renamed the Frank F. Fasi Municipal Building, as part of the Frank F. Fasi Civic Center.

Fasi served as Mayor for six terms over 22 years, and was responsible for many civic improvements, including this building, TheBus, satellite city halls, open markets, and the Honolulu City Lights celebration.

"Sky Gate"

1977

Isamu Noguchi, artist

In 1975, the National Endowment for the Arts (NEA) awarded the city a $50,000 matching grant for a sculpture to grace the entrance of the new Municipal Office Building (The Fasi Building).

Five finalists were chosen out of 109 applicants: Ken Shutt, Alexander Calder, Joseph Goto, Clement Meadmore, and the winner, Isamu Noguchi.

But there was a huge controversy since the NEA announced they wanted a different artist who had not even applied. The city finally prevailed.

But what you see today was not the winning design. After seeing the site, Noguchi decided to create something completely different he called the "Sky Gate". It cost $122,000 and was made in Cleveland.

Twice a year, at 12:28 pm on May 26th and 12:37 pm on July 16th, the sun is directly overhead in what is called the "Lahaina Noon", and the shadow of the curvy sculpture forms a perfect circle underneath.

MISSION MEMORIAL BUILDING

1916

Designed by architect Harry L. Kerr for the Hawaiian Evangelical Association, this building was built by the Lord-Young Engineering Company at a cost of $66,800 in 1916.

It was built on the site of the Kawaiahao Seminary and the Honolulu Mission Printing Office, and it is the only example of Neo-Classical Jeffersonian architecture in Hawaii. It was purchased by the city in 1945.

The Hawaii Evangelical Association is part of the Hawaiian Mission Children's Society of descendants of the first American Protestant missionaries who came to Hawaii in 1820.

The Hawaiian Mission Houses Historic Site is located directly across King Street.

"Nani I Ke Kumu"
LOOK TO THE SOURCE
1995

Michael Weidenbach, artist

This sculpture was named for the 2-volume book of traditional Hawaiian cultural practices and beliefs by Mary Kawena Pukui, E.W. Haertig and Catharine A. Lee, published by the Queen Liliuokalani Children's Center in 1972.

ḨAWAII ḼAW ÉNFORCEMENT ṀEMORIAL

2016

Honoring members of Honolulu's law enforcement agencies who have been killed in the line of duty, the Hawaii Law Enforcement Memorial was created through the tireless efforts of Joan Gribbin-Aiu.

Plaques on the walls name and honor each of the fallen officers.

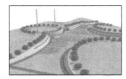

The design is the result of a competition sponsored by the School of Architecture at the University of Hawaii.

After 30 designs had been submitted, a jury of professors and local design professionals selected the five top designs. That was narrowed down to three semi-finalists whose 3D model designs were voted on by the 900 attendees of the 1st Annual Hawaii Law Enforcement Memorial Foundation's Gala Benefit on December 11, 2010.

The memorial was officially dedicated on May 15, 2016.

ᴋALANIMOKU ʙUILDING

1976

Formerly dedicated on March 31, 1976, this $13M building was designed by Shoso Kagawa, and houses a variety of state agencies.

It is named for Kalanimoku, the Prime Minister under Kamehameha I, II, and III.

During the design planning process, it was just called the State Office Building, or "SOB" which caused a few chuckles.

The blessing ceremony was disrupted by novelty and trinket saleswoman Ma Ma Loa shouting and rebuking the blessing until pure Hawaiians get the land, money, and respect they deserve.

The building is adjacent to what was once known as Printer's Lane, where John E. Bush, the "Napoleon of Printers' Lane" and publisher of the Ka Oiaio and Ka Leo o ka Lahui newspapers was charged with contempt in 1899 for ridiculing the Court. He was a staunch royalist and member of the "White Feather Brigade" and in 1894 was charged with conspiracy in a plot to overthrow the government.

Printer's Lane disappeared with the extension of Hotel Street to Alapai Street in 1902.

Honolulu Hale

1929

Known as City Hall, this Spanish Colonial Revival building was designed by a consortium of architects including Charles Dickey, Hart Wood, Guy Rothwell, John Kangeter, Marcus Lester, and Robert Miller.

> "They were of the opinion that the city hall for Honolulu should have individuality and charm that are suitable to the climate, and will be of great interest architecturally to visitors."

The building was built of reinforced concrete by Walker & Olund for $711,720. It is partly two stories and partly three stories, with a commanding tower on the Punchbowl Street side.

One of the main features is a large interior court with a monumental staircase in back, leading to a loggia on the second floor with city offices.

The columns, balconies, shields, and door frames were of art stone made from crushed Hawaiian sandstone by Mario Valdastri.

Although not quite completed, it officially opened for business to much fanfare on December 17, 1929.

Hawaii State Library

1913 / 1930

One of many libraries throughout the US that were funded by the generosity of steel magnate Andrew Carnegie, this building was designed by architect Henry D. Whitfield. The columns in front are a distinctive feature of all Carnegie libraries.

It was built on the site of the Pohukaina Girl's School for Native Hawaiians, located on Punchbowl Street from 1874 to 1912.

The library grew rapidly, and architect Charles W. Dickey was hired to design new wings on each side, creating a quadrangle with an open-air courtyard that was completed in 1930.

The library currently holds over 525,000 books, including an impressive Hawaii & Pacific section.

The front lawn is the site of the 2-story mansion of Honolulu manufacturer James A. Hopper, built in 1881 on the site of an earlier coral house which had a French 5-franc coin from 1832 in its cornerstone.

ℌawaii §tate 𝔄rchives

1906 / 1953

The Kanaʻaina Building was designed by architect Oliver G. Traphagen in 1906, and it was the original home of the Hawaii State Archives.

Mark Potter designed a new building in back in 1953, the one you see from the "Palace Walk". It is built on the site of the 1887 electric plant built by King Kalākaua to provide lights for the palace.

The Hawaii State Archives are the official repository of Hawaiian governmental history, yet they also have an amazing collection of historical artifacts and photographs, many of which can be viewed online.

ℋAWAII ℌTATE ℭAPITOL

1969

Perhaps the most unique capital building in the United States, the Hawaii State Capitol was designed by John Carl Warnecke along with Belt Lemon and Lo (Architects Hawaii Ltd) in a distinctly "Hawaiian International" style.

Governor John Burns specifically wanted the capitol to represent Hawaii's people, history, culture, and aloha.

The 40 columns that surround the building emulate palm trees, the reflecting pool that surrounds the building symbolizes the Pacific Ocean, and the two cone-shaped legislative chambers represent volcanoes. There is a large open atrium in the middle, and rainbows can sometimes be seen inside when it rains.

The building is on the original site of the Iolani Barracks, the Drill Shed, the Palace stables, and the original site of the Chief's Children's School.

Before constructing this building, the legislature met in Iolani Palace for over 70 years.

"THE SPIRIT OF LILI'UOKALANI"

1982

Marianna Pineda, artist

Commissioned by the State Legislature in 1975, this statue of Her Majesty Lydia Liliu Loloku Walania Wewehi Kamakeohaa Kapaakea, otherwise known as Queen Lili'uokalani, was cast in Boston and officially dedicated on April 10, 1982.

In her left hand she holds the sheet music to "Aloha Oe", a page from the 1893 Hawaii Constitution, and the ancient creation chant known as the Kumulipo.

Some say she was deliberately placed here to keep an eye on the legislature!

ɪOLANI ᑭALACE

1882

Iolani Palace is without a doubt the most important building in Honolulu and Hawaii, and it is the only Royal Palace in the United States.

> *"'Iolani Palace is a living restoration of a proud Hawaiian national identity and is recognized as the spiritual and physical multicultural epicenter of Hawai'i"*

'Iolani means the "hawk", or "bird of heaven".

It was built for King Kalākaua, and the cornerstone was laid on Queen Kapiolani's birthday, December 31, 1879, with full Masonic pageantry.

The architect was Australian-born Thomas J. Baker, who also designed and built the first Bishop Bank on Merchant Street, the Benson-Smith Building at Fort and Hotel streets, and the Dillingham Building on Fort Street that had the first freight elevator.

The brick and stonework were by Englishman E.B. "Ted" Thomas, and the woodwork was by George Lucas from County Clare in Ireland.

The building is 140' x 120' with an 80' tall tower, in a style considered to be "American Florentine".

Baker quarreled with the Minister of the Interior over project authority, so he was paid $1000 and replaced by Charles J. Wall who was eventually fired for having trouble getting timely shipments from the US mainland. The final architect was Isaac Moore.

Although not quite finished, King Kalākaua spent his first night in the new palace on November 15, 1882.

The first public event was a Grand Masonic Banquet on December 27, 1882.

The Palace was officially opened up for public inspection at a Palace Garden Party on June 26, 1884, "thus affording a rare opportunity for residents and strangers to visit the finest residence in the Kingdom."

The grounds were enclosed with an 8'-high stone wall with wooden gates, and later iron gates.

After visiting with Thomas Edison in New York, King Kalākaua had 325 incandescent lights installed in the palace in 1887, powered by a 100 hp engine onsite. This was four years before lights were installed in the White House in Washington, D.C.

Liliʻuokalani became queen on January 20, 1891 upon the death of her brother, King Kalākaua.

The Kingdon of Hawaii was overthrown on January 17, 1893, by a group of 13 businessmen who called themselves the Committee of Safety. What they were mostly interested in saving was their sugar profits and their hopes of annexation to the United States.

Queen Liliʻuokalani was placed under house arrest and although there were attempts to restore the monarchy, they were ultimately unsuccessful.

After 1893 the palace was known as the Executive Building and it was the headquarters for the Provisional Government as well as for the Republic, Territory, and State of Hawaii until the new capitol building was completed in 1969.

In 1903 there were plans to expand the building with designs for additional wings submitted by Howard and Train, and Newcomb and Dickey. Luckily, the plans never happened.

FRONT VIEW OF CAPITOL BUILDING SHOWING BOTH WINGS.

FRONT VIEW FROM KING STREET, SHOWING PALACE AND NEW WING.

There was a previous Iolani Palace on this site...

Beginning in 1840 with the gathering of materials for a stone palace, Governor Kekuanaoʻa started construction on a Greek-revival structure in July 1844 that was a 1-story coral building, 74' x 44', with a high basement, a wide veranda all around, and a "lookout" room on top of the roof.

Lith. of Britton & Rey. PALACE OF KING KAMEHAMEHA III. Published by Paul Emmert

Called Hanailoia, meaning "the prediction of things to come", it was designed and built by Capt. Isaac S. Hart, and was said to be "the grandest home in Honolulu" and "by far the most costly and imposing dwelling which has been erected here".

In 1845, Kamehameha III moved the government to Honolulu from Lahaina and the palace officially opened on February 4, 1845, with a grand soiree, along with public receptions on the following Thursdays for soldiers and students and notable kamaainas. It was renamed ʻIolani Palace in 1863.

In traditional Hawaiian aliʻi style, it had a throne room, reception room, and state dining room, but no sleeping rooms – they were located in nearby cottages, as were kitchen and bathing facilities.

King Kalākaua entrusted Archibald Cleghorn to fix up the building while he was away but an inspection showed "the entire woodwork was too far decayed" and "impracticable to repair" so it was demolished in 1874.

This gate along Palace Walk was added in 1883 as a back exit so Queen Liliʻuokalani's husband, John Owen Dominis, could easily travel back and forth to their residence at Washington Place.

If you had been standing in this exact spot on the afternoon of July 30, 1889, at 5:30 pm, there would have been incendiary bombs flying over your head.

Over 30 revolutionaries led by Robert Wilcox were holed up in the Royal Bungalow (where the Iolani Barracks are today), and although they were able to hold the government at bay for several hours, they were eventually dislodged due to the strong arm of baseball player James Hay Wodehouse who hid behind the Coney House on the mauka side of Palace Walk and successfully lobbed several bombs into the Royal Bungalow until Wilcox and his men surrendered.

Immediately after the insurrection, the palace walls, called "a relic of the Middle Ages", were reduced from 8' high to 3'-6".

The decorative iron fence of "ornamental pickets with fancy posts" came from Champion Iron Fence in Kenton, OH, and was installed in 1892 by the Pacific Hardware Company for $7,063.

ỊOLANI ฿ARRACKS

1871

Also known as Hale Koa, the Iolani Barracks of the Royal Guard were designed by German-born architect Theodore C. Heuck and completed in 1871.

They were originally located about 600' away, where the Punchbowl Street side of the State Capitol is today. It was carefully dismantled and reconstructed here in 1965.

Hawaii State Archives

The Royal Bungalow, built in 1883, was previously on this site until 1918. It was a favorite relaxation place for King Kalākaua and Queen Kapiolani.

ᴛHE ⒪VERTHROW OF THE ᴍONARCHY

In spite of having barracks and soldiers nearby, the Kingdom of Hawaii was overthrown on January 17, 1893, by a group of capitalists and lawyers who called themselves the Committee of Safety, led by Sanford B. Dole.

They were concerned about tariffs impacting the lucrative sugar industry, as well as their ultimate goal of annexation to the United States.

With marines from the *USS Boston* standing by, the Committee instigated their coup, commandeered Iolani Palace, and deposed Queen Lili'uokalani who was kept in the palace under house arrest.

Many countries over the years had previously attempted to take control of the Hawaiian Islands, including renegade Russians, French, and English. But the British government always supported the Hawaiian monarchy and this resulted in the Union Jack being incorporated into the upper left corner (the "canton") of the Hawaiian Flag.

Adopted in 1845, it is the only US state flag that features a foreign country's national flag.

Korean-Vietnam War Memorial

1994

In 1990, 81 entries were submitted in a juried design competition led by architect Vladimir Ossipoff for a Korean and Vietnam War Memorial. But the winning design by two city employees was so strongly opposed by local veterans that five members of the commission resigned, losing its quorum.

A new competition was held in 1992, and out of 51 entries the selected design was by local architect Paul Medley with Fritz Johnson Architects.

Dedicated on July 24, 1994, it has 758 names from the two wars, inscribed on black granite pedestals on two low serpentine moss walls.

A large stone church once stood on the grassy site across from Washington Place – the Central Union Church, built in 1892. When the church moved farther out on Beretania Street in 1924, the building was purchased by the Schuman Carriage Company and turned into an automobile showroom – possibly the only automobile showroom in the world with stained glass windows!

RICHARDS STREET

Hawaiian Mission Children's Society

Richards Street was named for former missionary and later King's Minister of Public Instruction and President of the Board of Commissioners, Reverend William Richards.

He was born on August 22, 1793, at Plainfield, MA, and after graduating from Williams College, he arrived in Hawaii as a missionary on April 27, 1823.

He was instrumental in framing the Constitution of 1840, and he was a member of the embassy to the United States, Great Britain, and France in 1842/43 that helped insure the independence of the Kingdom of Hawaii.

CAPITOL MODERN

THE HAWAII STATE ART MUSEUM

250 S. Hotel
1928

This 5-story concrete building was designed by Lincoln Rogers from San Diego along with local architects Emory & Webb as the new building for the Army and Navy YMCA.

It cost $600,000 and was officially dedicated on March 16, 1928. It had 268 sleeping rooms, a swimming pool, billiard hall, cafeteria, barbershop, gymnasium, auditorium, tailor, and curio shops. It was the major R&R hub for Pacific military personnel during World War II.

It was built on the site of the Hawaiian Hotel, also known as the Royal Hawaiian Hotel.

"His Majesty's cabinet took the initiative and on December 5, 1870, adopted a resolution authorizing the erection of the hotel and the issue of bonds to the amount of $100,000 for this object."

Local citizens raised an additional $42,500 and foundation excavation work began on May 15, 1870.

The land, including iron fence, building, furniture, fixtures, bedding, etc. cost a total of $134,027.65.

The Hawaiian Hotel was completed by the end of 1871 but was not formally opened until February 1872 due to delays in getting furniture.

In the first 14 months of operation over 2,000 names were recorded in the hotel registry "from nearly every country in the world".

Hawaii State Archives

The building had two wings connected by a central section with 10-foot-wide "verandahs" on the mauka and makai sides. It had 48 sleeping rooms and 10 other general rooms, with concrete walls in a "rustic finish, similar to that of the new Post Office". It was built by J.G. Osborne with direction and oversight provided by C.H. Lewers.

It became the Army and Navy YMCA in 1917.

Hawaii State Archives

The architectural details of the current building were inspired by the Davanzatti Palace in Florence, Italy, and the design also included an homage to the previous hotel's large circular lanais added in 1899.

It became the Hawaii State Art Museum in 2002.

Honolulu's Royal Mile

ALI'I PLACE

1099 Alakea
1992

Described as Honolulu's finest example of "Postmodern historicism", the $91M 23-story Ali'i Place office tower with 9-story 1,000-car parking garage was designed by David Hart of Daniel Mann Johnson & Mendenhall (DMJM) and completed by Nordic/Mortenson in 1992.

The 9'x 16' entrance mural is by Yvonne Cheng.

In the late 1800's this was the site of the extensive Hawaiian Hotel Stables, and later the Hawaiian Hotel Garage and the Von Hamm-Young Garage.

Black Cat Café (site)

239 S. Hotel
1901 – c.1968

Hawaiian Time Machine

This 2-story wooden building was built in 1901 as the Hotel Stables with stalls for 54 horses, becoming the Royal Hawaiian Garage with automobiles for sale and for hire in 1908.

In 1930, Donald F. Darrow and Stanley Shaughnessy opened the Black Cat Café, known by virtually every G.I. in Hawaii in World War II. It was directly across the street from the Army and Navy YMCA, and next to the bus and taxi stands connecting downtown Honolulu with Schofield Barracks and Pearl Harbor.

Sailors lined up for blocks to see the hula girls and pretty waitresses, and to enjoy the menu featuring 15 cent hamburgers and 10 cent hot dogs.

The site today is the Aliʻi Place fountain courtyard.

ᒍ ARVES 卅 OUSE (SITE)

209 S. Hotel
c.1840 – 1919

On the mauka/waikiki corner stood the 2-story coral stone house of James Jackson Jarves, likely built around 1840 and demolished in 1919.

Jarves was the editor of *The Polynesian* newspaper from 1840 to 1848, and the author of the landmark book the *History of the Hawaiian or Sandwich Islands* published in 1843.

Jarves moved to Florence, Italy, in the 1850's and served as vice-consul while becoming a renowned international art connoisseur, author, and collector.

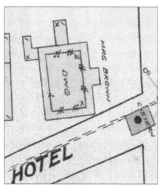

𝔇istrict 𝔠ourt 𝔅uilding

1111 Alakea
1982

In spite of the City Planning Commission voting 5-1 against it, the brutalist-style 11-story District Court Building ("Kauikeaouli Hale") was designed by Anbe, Aruga & Ishizu Architects, Inc. and completed in 1982 at a cost of $24M.

It is on the site of a castle-like Masonic Temple designed by Clinton B. Ripley in the Richardsonian Romanesque style that was built in 1893.

Hawaii State Archives

The cornerstone with time capsule was laid on December 27, 1892, to much pomp and ceremony, including multiple speeches and rituals, the St. Andrews Cathedral choir, and the Hawaiian Band. Queen Lili'uokalani was in attendance as was Governor Cleghorn and four Ministers of the Crown.

Known as the Aloha Building by the 1960's, the former temple was demolished in 1967.

Hawaii State Archives

The Masonic Temple was built on the site of the Royal Hawaiian Theatre which opened on June 24, 1848, with the Prize Address delivered by Charley Vincent, a performance of the Highland Fling, and the comedy "She Stoops to Conquer".

The theatre building was demolished in June 1881.

> ☞ The "Royal Hawaiian Theatre" is demolished. The little temple, cor. of Hotel and Alakea streets, where Biscacianti, Madame States, the Carandinis, Florence Colville, and others in past times, and recently the Wells Troupe,delighted Honolulu theatre goers, is now a mass of building debris ; and the present proprietor Dr. McGrew is about to erect a new structure, for public amusement or for other purposes possibly, not yet determined.

"BEAR AND CUBS"

1984

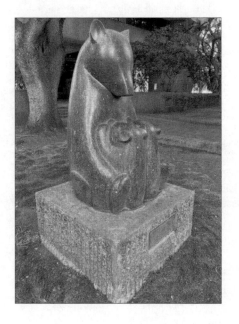

Beniamino Bufano, artist

Installed in front of the District Court Building, this black granite sculpture was created by famed San Francisco artist Beniamino Bufano (1890-1970).

ALAKEA STREET

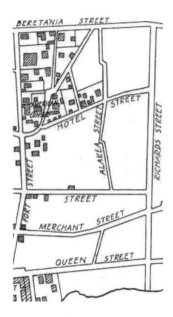

Alakea Street was first known as Cross Street, then White Street, which translated into Hawaiian is "alakea" and presumably named for the white coral rock it was initially paved with.

It started out as a crooked little lane of variable width at the edge of the posh foreigners housing area, but by 1889 it had been widened enough for the Hawaiian Tramways Company to run mule-driven streetcars on it "20 minutes past each hour" between 6:20 am and 9:20 pm.

First YMCA Building
(SITE)

185-195 S. Hotel / 1092 Alakea
1883 – 1946

The first building on this site was the "fine large straw house" of Judge George Morison Robertson. An 8-room 1-story wooden house was built here in December 1853 at a cost of $5,400. It was the residence of David L. Gregg, U.S. Commissioner.

Hawaii State Archives

In 1883, the YMCA built their first building at this corner, adding a gymnasium in 1895. It was purchased in 1911 by Elks Lodge B.P.O.E. 616, and they later leased it to the YWCA.

In 1943 it became the Hawaiian Midway amusement center for sailors. It was demolished in 1946.

ᴀ̶lakea ᴄorporate ᴛower

1100 Alakea

1993

The 31-story office tower called Alakea Corporate Tower was designed by Stringer Tusher & Associates and built for automobile dealer James Pflueger in 1993.

It replaced the Merchandise Mart, purchased in 1945 for $353,000 at public auction and later remodeled and "modernized".

But it was once a beautiful big new YMCA building, designed by Ripley & Reynolds and built in 1911. It was "designed for tropical life" around an interior courtyard, and featured a dramatic corner entry that was the winner of a design competition.

Hawaii State Archives

This new YMCA building had two cornerstones. The time capsule of the old YMCA across the street was removed and opened in 1911, and then combined with the contents of the new time capsule. The new cornerstone was inscribed with the territorial motto "Ua ma uke ea o ka aina i ka pono".

This new YMCA building replaced the Honolulu Library and Reading Room built in 1883.

Hawaii State Archives

The adobe cottage of George Pelly, agent of the Hudson's Bay Company, was built at the corner with Adams Lane 1830's and was surrounded by a high stone wall. The Pelly premises were used as government offices from 1854 to 1862.

ℨℂ HOTEL BY MARRIOTT

1111 Bishop
1964

In 2024, a new AC Marriott hotel opened in the former Investors Finance building designed by Ernest Hara and constructed in 1964.

For nearly 65 years this was the site of the coolest (and sweetest) building in downtown Honolulu – the Elite Ice Cream Parlor and Candy Factory, from 1899 to 1964.

Known as the Elite Building, it was designed by Oliver Traphagen and it replaced a wooden dentist office. Traphagen designed three versions of an ornate new 3-story building – terra cotta and pressed brick, same but with galvanized cornice and stucco, or blue stone and stucco.

JAS. STEINER'S NEW BUILDING, CORNER HOTEL STREET AND ADAMS LANE. PLANS BY TRAPHAGEN.

The selected design was pressed brick and terra cotta imported from Italy, in a highly ornamented Italian Renaissance style with "Elite 1899" incorporated into the main cornice.

The first floor and basement housed the Elite Restaurant run by Hart & Co., 12 offices were on the second floor, and the third floor had a large meeting hall with a 15-foot ceiling with three ornamental domes 12 feet in diameter.

James Steiner divided the downstairs into three stores in 1907 to accommodate his very successful Island Curios business.

Steiner was born in Austria in 1860 and came to Hawaii when he was 22 years old. He worked for candy makers Hart Brothers, caterers to Hawaiian royalty. He later became partner and sole owner.

In the early 1950's, Gibson's Bar was on the second floor of the "tawdry, fancy-fronted Elite Building". It had "murals in circus colors of sailors chasing hula girls in grass skirts, of Princess Pupule with plenty papaya, of Manuela Boy with a big opu", and it also featured live Dixieland jazz.

Located immediately behind the building was the house of Capt. Alexander Adams, built before 1850.

Born in Arbroath, Scotland, in 1780, Captain Adams served in the British Royal Navy and came to Hawaii in 1810. He quickly became the trusted commander of King Kamehameha's sandalwood fleet and was also one of three pilots for the Honolulu harbor.

Hard to believe, but Adams Lane and the other streets in this area were once narrow little leafy lanes lined with picket fences in front of the wood and coral homes of Honolulu's wealthy foreigners.

§CULPTURE

1983

Sean Browne, artist

This granite sculpture By Native Hawaiian artist Sean Browne was installed in memory of Fred Kresser, President of the Pacific Construction Company, the builders of the Bishop Square Pauahi Tower. Kresser was one of seven people tragically killed in Singapore on January 29, 1983, when a floating oil rig hit the cable car they were riding in.

In 1988, Browne was commissioned by the Oahu Imin Kanyaku Centennial Commission to create a life-size statue of King Kalākaua, which now stands proudly at the junction of Kalākaua and Kuhio avenues in Waikiki.

𝔅ISHOP 𝔖QUARE

1001 Bishop
1983

The 28-story Pauahi Tower and Tamarind Park of Bishop Square were designed by Franklin Gray and Chapman Cobeen Desai & Sakata along with landscape artist James C. Hubbard. It was named in honor of Bernice Pauahi Bishop who had formerly lived on this site, and it was completed in 1983.

It replaced the massive Alexander Young Building that covered half the block along Bishop Street.

Hawaii State Archives

The Alexander Young Hotel and Office Building was designed by George W. Percy and Henry H. Meyers, and completed in 1903.

Bishop Street was created as the frontage for the building, and when first built only ran between King Street and Hotel Street.

The Young Building was the largest building built in Hawaii up to that date, with an estimated cost of $750,000. The mauka end was the hotel and the makai end housed offices and shops. Its roof garden was known worldwide.

The 75,000 pieces of iron and steel for the building came from the Milliken Brothers in New York City and were shipped around Cape Horn on the steamships *Hawaiian* and *Oregonian*.

The large stone blocks for the foundation were cut in California by John D. McGilvray and brought on the 4-masted schooner *Rosamond* and the schooner *Mary E. Foster*; some were the largest ever brought to Hawaii, weighing up to seven tons apiece.

The hotel had 192 rooms, with $25,000 in mahogany and oak furniture from Grand Rapids, Michigan, personally selected by manager H. Wingate Lake and shipped around The Horn.

Alexander Young was born in Blackburn, Scotland, in 1832. Initially working in Glasgow and London, he went to Vancouver in 1860 to build a sawmill.

In 1865, he and his family came to Hawaii where he later became the manager of the Honolulu Iron Works and the owner of several sugar companies.

Hawaii State Archives

From 1887 to 1892, Young served in the House of Nobles and was briefly the Minister of the Interior from late 1899 to mid-1900.

In 1899, Young created the von Hamm-Young Company with his son Archibald Young and new son-in-law Conrad von Hamm, selling automobiles and developing the Alexander Young Building.

The hotel rooms were converted into offices in 1969 as hotel demand moved to Waikiki.

Although listed on the National Register of Historic Places, Northwest Mutual Life Insurance Company decided to demolish the building in 1981 in spite of community protests and an emergency restraining order from the Hawaii Supreme Court.

All efforts failed, and demolition began July 7, 1981.

The Alexander Young Building was on the site of Dr. Robert Wood's large coral house on Hotel Street that was built in 1847. Dr. Wood came to Hawaii from Boston to practice medicine. He sold the house to Dr. John McGrew in 1866. Dr. McGrew had come to Hawaii to help recover from the Civil War.

The McGrews were famous for their hospitality and the mansion hosted many social events for politicians and dignitaries. It was decorated with curios from the Orient and had a suite of heavy oak furniture that had belonged to Louis XVIII.

The house was described as:

> "a large, square house, standing alone, built of gray coral blocks, pointed with white cement, two stories high, surrounded on each side by a wide veranda over which juts the peaked roof. No chimneys mar it. The rooms are large and lofty. The doors and windows open upon the verandas, and command views of grass, flowers and trees. Between the cottage and the street is a fountain of water, surrounded by large-leafed, tropical plants, sea shell and roses".

Hawaii State Archives

The McGrews lived in this house for 34 years until retiring and selling the property in 1900 to Alexander Young for $150,000.

ℬISHOP ℛTREET

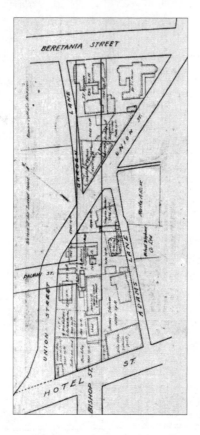

Bishop Street was not one of the original downtown streets – it was constructed in 1900 and named for Charles R. Bishop since it cut through his property to provide frontage for the Alexander Young Building. Initially only running between Hotel and King streets, it was extended to the harbor in 1918 and to Beretania Street in 1927.

The extension to Beretania resulted in the loss of Garden Lane, many buildings, and created two separate pieces of Union Street.

EXECUTIVE CENTER

1088 Bishop
1983

The $129M Executive Center was a massive project designed by Jo Paul Rognstad for developer L. Robert Allen that demolished all but two buildings on the block for two proposed 40-story mirrored-glass towers with a 10-story parking garage.

The second tower never happened due to open space and floor area issues, and Allen ended up facing involuntary Chapter 7 bankruptcy.

The tower replaced the first Long's Drug Store in Hawaii, built in 1954. Long's was founded by Joseph M. & Tom Long in Oakland, California in 1938.

The Long's Drug Store building was the site of the Richard W. Laine residence, a 1-story frame house here from at least 1885 to 1899. Laine was the Spanish Vice-Consul to Hawaii in 1880 and later the Consul for Mexico.

ⓄREGON ⒷLOCK

148-162 S. Hotel / 1113-1119 Union
1901, 1927

This building is a fragment of its former self, as the extension of Bishop Street in late 1926 plowed right through the middle of the original 1901 structure. Herbert Cayton designed the 1927 reconfiguration.

Bishop Museum

When first built, the Oregon Block was a 2-story brick building with 7 stores, built in 1901 by Victor Hoffman and John F. Riley.

Initially called the Hibernia Block, it was built on the site of the Fashion Stables and Fire Engine House No.2. The Portland Building was added in the corner at Hotel and Union streets in 1903.

ℙortland 𝔹uilding

134-S. Hotel / 1109 Union
1903

Hawaii State Archives

If you are wondering why this is called the Portland Building, it is because it was built into a corner notch left out of the 1901 Oregon Block.

Hawaii State Archives

Auditor and stockbroker J.H. Fisher had to wait for a Chinese store's lease to run out, and he was finally able to build on this tiny lot in 1903. Its first tenant was a cigar store with a private room up above.

This corner was previously the location of the Fashion Stables from 1881 to 1894.

Hawaii State Archives

NEW OPENING!!
BISMARK'S
FASHION STABLES!

No. 3 Union St., next to No. 2 Engine Co., and No. 93 Hotel St.

Express Nos. 7, 9, 32, 34, 53, 91, 193,

First Class Horses and Carriages

To Rent at any Hour of the Day or Night.

All Orders Promptly Attended to.

Telephone No. 148.   Terms Reasonable.

Particular attention paid to Boarding Horses by the Day, Week or Month.   oc29 tf

Hawaii State Archives

In this photograph by H.L. Chase from 1870, it looks like the corner was a residence next to the fire station and belltower.

But by 1879 it was the office and harness room of the Bismark livery stable.

Union Street Mall

Union Street was initially called Alanui Maua, Alanui Huina, Keʻekeʻe, Branch Street, and Crooked Lane, but was known as Union Street as early as 1851.

According to Mrs. Monsarrat, Union Street was named for a street in her English hometown and it was in the heart of the early mostly foreigner residential area.

Instigated by the Downtown Improvement Association, the section of Union Street between Hotel and Bishop streets was turned into a pedestrian shopping mall in 1964, the first in Honolulu. It had greenery, benches, and a drinking fountain, and cost $43,000.

At the time there was a lot of retail on Union Street, including a large 3-story Kress store. Today it is essentially a bus stop waiting area and large public sidewalk with little to no retail, with storefronts subjected to crime and vandalism.

In the mid-1800's the street was also the location of the French Hotel, the Monsarrat and Dowsett houses, plus Fire Station No.2 and the fire alarm Bell Tower.

Bell Tower & Fire Station (Site)

1109-Union
1870 – 1900

The Fire Engine House of Mechanic Company No.2 was located here just off Hotel Street.

In 1857 they erected a tall flagpole "surmounted with a gilt Vulcan's arm" displaying a new red flag with the words "Mechanic 2" in white letters.

Hawaii State Archives

They added a 75' tall hexagonal Alarm Bell Tower in 1870 that was designed and built by James Renton. The bell was cast in Troy, New York, weighed 1,018 pounds, and cost $500.

The landmark tower was demolished in 1900 after 30 years of service.

OLD BELL TOWER BEING TORN DOWN

Building Housed Honolulu's Fire Department in Olden Days. Hibernia Block.

The old Bell Tower building on Union street is being demolished. The tumble-down structures, weatherbeaten and dilapidated, have been standing for the last thirty years, unoccupied of late except as a carpenter shIp. In their time the buildings, and especially the one surmounted by a towering fire belfry, were quite an ornament to old Honolulu.

When first erected the buildings were used by the volunteer fire department and the hook and ladder and an engine were housed there. In the tall tower the fire bell was hung and a watchman gazed from its heights during the night-time to detect the first signs of a fire. Later, when the building began to show signs of age, the steeple became unsafe and was cut down to the proportions of a small-sized cupola and the bell was removed, fire signals being given by a deep-voiced siren along the waterfront.

As soon as the buildings are razed, excavation work will be commenced on the site. The residence cottage now standing on the Ewa side of the new Elite building, on Hotel street, will also be razed. The new Hibernia building, when erected, will thus have the advantage of two fine frontages, one on Hotel street and the other where the Bell Tower buildings now are. The corner property will not be touched for the present. The Hibernia block will be a fitting companion to the artistic Elite block, just finished.

The Honolulu Advertiser, May 4, 1900

Palm Building

116-118 S. Hotel

1912

Hidden behind a 1964 "modernization" is the Palm Café Building built in 1912. If you look closely at the second floor, the original building is barely visible between the slats of the latter-day remuddling.

The first floor of the Palm Café housed the confectionary and bakery business in front with a dining room at the back, and a broad stairway led to more restaurant space upstairs.

In 1927 it became the home of Thayer's Piano Company and music store.

Leonard E. Thayer came to Hawaii in 1905 with 30 years' experience in the piano business plus a stock of Steinway pianos.

The Thayer's music store was in the Palm Building for over 50 years.

𝔅ENSON 𝔖MITH 𝔅UILDING
(SITE)

1063-1071 Fort / 101-107 S. Hotel
1877 – 1954

This corner was the site of the Robert Davis dry goods store in the 1840's, and it was the location of the Family Market by the 1860's.

The market building was moved out of the way along Hotel Street in 1868 so Archibald S. Cleghorn could build a new 26' x 36' wooden store. His dry goods store was here from 1869 to 1877.

Charles Brewer from Boston hired Thomas J. Baker to build a new 2-story brick building here in 1877.

Hawaii State Archives

In 1885, the three stores in the building were Goo Kim, Thomas G. Thrum, and N.S. Sachs.

For nearly 60 years, from June 1894 to December 30, 1953, the corner was the Benson Smith Drug Store.

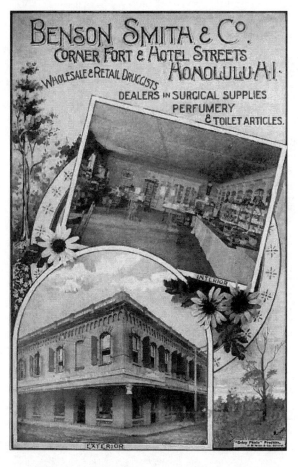

The building was demolished in 1954 for a new 3-story F.W. Woolworth Store, which was demolished in 1981 for the $129M Executive Center.

Fort Street Mall

The Honolulu Fort, also known as Kekuanohu ("back of the scorpion fish"), was established in 1817, and had 52 guns that were never fired in anger.

Fort Street extended mauka from the front gate of the fort, and it was the premier retail location in Honolulu until August 13, 1959 – the day the Ala Moana Center opened 1.5 miles away with 80 stores and acres of free parking.

In a desperate attempt to compete, the city decided to convert Fort Street into a pedestrian-only shopping mall, as was the fashion with many other mainland cities at the time.

After 9 months of disruptive construction, the Fort Street Mall was formally dedicated on February 22, 1969.

The mall is 5 blocks long (1,738'), 50' wide, and had a pedestrian underpass at King Street. The total construction cost was $2,766,484.50.

At the time it was created there were 53 retail establishments along the route, plus a major bank, 4 savings & loan associations, a hotel, offices, and a cathedral.

"Paved in brick with a pattern of cement dividers, the mall contains 37 specially designed overhead light fixtures that also include a high fidelity sound system, 45 wood and concrete benches, 20 planters, two fountains, a large pool, a waterfall, a children's sandbox, and a large (70-by-9 foot) mural that is a major work of art."

"Landscaping includes an avenue of 58 'false olive' trees accented in various spots with five coral trees, four coco palms, four scarlet bottlebrush, three rainbow showers, two golden showers, and one monkeypod, in addition to numberous flowers, green plants, vines and grasses."

As suburbs and the automobile continued to grow in popularity, the Fort Street Mall began to lose its luster and many of the business who had multiple locations eventually closed their stores on Fort Street.

Today it is more of a pedestrian path between office buildings than shopping mecca. Stores continue to struggle, especially post-pandemic, but it is hoped the renewed interest in downtown residential projects will bring new life and new purpose.

Mott-Smith Building

1101-1103 Fort / 102-110 S. Hotel
1885

This building takes the grand prize for the greatest number of remodels in its 140-year history – at least eight that we know of. But the big question is, has any of the original 1885 building survived?

There's a lot to unpack here, so let's start at the beginning...

This area was originally part of a giant yam field that helped provision visiting ships.

The first recorded building was the dentist office of John Mott-Smith here by 1856, shared with Dr. William Hillebrand.

In 1878, Mott-Smith leased the building to the California One Price Bazar, owned by Charles J. Fishel and Alfred M. Mellis. And yes, that's how they spelled it.

Fishel enlarged the building in 1882 and it became Charles J. Fishel's Popular Store. Fishel was born in Trieste, Italy, in 1853, and was one of Honolulu's most prosperous Jewish merchants.

Hawaii State Archives

Just after midnight on January 20, 1885, a fire started in the back of Fishel's store that swept through the makai end of the block and destroyed Fishel's building and several others.

Fishel quickly rebuilt, hiring George Lucas to erect a 1-story brick building in 1885, but he quickly decided to make it 2 stories. It had two of the largest plate glass windows in the city, and by September the sign writer was adding the final "artistic touches".

The grand opening included Chinese lanterns, an exhibition, and a concert by the Royal Hawaiian Band.

Hawaiian Historical Society

In 1894, Fishel planned to return to New York City so he sold out his stock and leased the building to L.E. Tracy who moved here from his previous store on King Street.

The upstairs was used by the Scottish Thistle Club and the Japanese Methodist Episcopal Church. Tracy installed an electric sign on the front of the store in 1894, perhaps the first in Hawaii.

Photographer Frank Davey opened a photographic gallery upstairs in January 1897.

Born in London in 1860, he had been the manager and chief operator of the Taber Photograph Gallery in San Francisco, and previously with Wallery of Paris and Van Der Weyde of London. His father was the famous English artist and engraver William Turner Davey.

FRANK DAVEY,
President Davey Photograph Co.

The Mott-Smith Estate bought back the lease in January of 1897 and hired Ripley & Dickey to design an "extensive remodeling" of the building that included removing 7 feet off the Fort Street side to accommodate the future street widening, making the exterior front and side "more modern", adding a third story, and a first for Hawaii – an electric passenger elevator.

The Kash store opened their second location here in 1899, specializing in "gents' furnishing goods and ready to wear clothing".

The building underwent extensive alterations again in 1906, combining the two exterior store entrances and adding a "spacious stairway" between the first and second floors while keeping the elevator.

Clifford Spitzer bought the building in late 1926 and it became The Hub after an additional remodeling.

The Mau family bought Hub Clothing from J.S. Spitzer in 1947, and "in line with the general facelifting of downtown stores and office buildings in recent years", embarked on an ambitious remodel in 1955 that included adding a giant 8' electric outdoor clock to the building.

Hub Clothing closed in 1980 and was replaced by a McDonald's restaurant.

McDonald's first location was two buildings mauka at 1113 Fort Street in 1972.

For the first year this new location was known as "McDonald's The Hub".

JAMES CAMPBELL BUILDING

1064-1072 Fort / 85 S. Hotel
1877, 1882, 1918

Hawaii State Archives

Although outwardly known as the James Campbell Building designed by Emory & Webb and completed in 1918, it is actually a combination of three different buildings, some dating back to 1877, that have been combined and reworked into the present building.

Portions of the older buildings might still exist on the inside, hard to tell.

The shop of "armourer" John Colcord was on this corner as early as 1841, and it was later the saddle and upholstery shop of J.P. Hughes from 1860 to 1869.

From 1870 to 1877 it was H.L. Chase's Cosmopolitan Photographic Gallery and studio, adjoining the Grunwald & Schutte dry goods store.

The wooden building was destroyed by a disastrous fire on March 18, 1877.

The large skylight visible in the photograph was for Chase's camera room.

After the fire, Thomas J. Baker built a 1-story building for C.E. Williams on the corner in 1877.

The tailor store of Henry Tregloan from Cornwall, England, was a mainstay of this corner for 24 years and the building was known as the Tregloan Building.

James Campbell purchased all of C.E. Williams' Honolulu properties in October 1877 for $50,000, and it is very likely he added the second floor when he was constructing the adjacent 2-story building on Hotel Street in 1882.

The Palmer & Thacher drug store was here in 1883, later bought out by Benson, Smith & Co., who relocated across the street in 1894.

Honolulu Photo Supply was here from 1900 to 1902.

The 1882 James Campbell Building was on the Hotel Street side and housed the retail store of S. Magnin and the grocery firm of Kennedy & Co. which became Lewis & Co. grocers in 1884.

The 1882 Campbell building was on the site of the cabinet-making shop of R.A.S. Wood and William C. Parke that was here as early as 1847.

Wood became sole owner in 1850 and sold the business to William Henry Stuart and Gustave W. Rahe in 1851.

It became Charles E. Williams cabinet-making shop in 1859.

Paul Emmert

The Williams/Hollister Building adjacent on the Fort Street side was also incorporated into the 1918 James Campbell Building.

The 1918 plans included remodeling the front of the 1872 Williams/Hollister Building and adding a third story while adding a basement and completely rebuilding the 1877/1882 Tregloan Building and 1882 Campbell Building on the Hotel Street side. Designed for 5 floors, only 3 were constructed.

ℙANTHEON ℬUILDING

1102-1122 Fort / 76-92 S. Hotel
1911

Hard to believe, but there was once a beautiful Italian Renaissance building at this corner that was covered up and/or destroyed with this 1964 attempt at "modernization".

James L. Young was credited as the architect of the 1911 building, but the design is virtually identical to a plan drawn by Harry L. Kerr in 1909.

It was originally planned as the front to the Art Theater Auditorium in back, but when that project fell through, the building was redesigned to eliminate the central entrance arcade from the Fort/Hotel Street corner.

For many years this corner was the site of the Pantheon Saloon owned by former circus strongman James Dodd from Belfast, Ireland. Also a Civil War veteran, Dodd was described as "public spirited and charitable, a good business man".

Dodd built a new building at the corner in 1883 that was lavishly decorated by two French artists, Lucien Buchmann and Fritz Rupprecht.

On February 7, 1900, the Pantheon Saloon and the adjoining stables were burned by the Board of Health in an attempt to limit the spread of the bubonic plague.

John G. Munn had a store on this corner as early as 1844, and by 1869 the large adobe building was the Bartlett Saloon, run by John Bartlett who had been the proprietor of the Canton Hotel in the 1850's.

Hawaii State Archives

In October 1878, James Dodd leased the Bartlett House and renamed it the Pantheon Hotel.

OPENING.—Mr. James Dodd has leased the premises known as the Bartlett House, at the corner of Hotel and Fort streets, to be called hereafter the Pantheon Hotel. The premises have been renovated, repaired, painted and papered throughout, making them look almost as good as new. Mr. Dodd has had experience in the hotel business, and from his urbanity of manner and good business habits we doubt not but the new place will be well kept. He intends to have, in connection with the hotel, a finely arranged livery stable with a full complement of carriages and saddle horses for the accommodation of the public. This latter arrangement will be a great convenience, and we hope Mr. D. will be well supported in both undertakings.

Hawaiian Gazette, October 30, 1878

Warren Hotel (site)

1008-1024 Fort
c.1825 – 1909

The Warren Hotel was opened in the 1820's by Major William R. Warren on the mauka side of Hotel Street, where the National Building sits today. This is where Hotel Street gets its name.

Known as "The Major" with a "big paunch, red face, and blonde eyebrows", Warren came to Hawaii before the missionaries arrived, and was in the hotel business by 1817.

Warren House was renowned for its food, here described in a poem composed and published upon Major Warren's impending departure to California in 1838:

> Cups of coffee quaff'd at ease,
> Legs of mutton, eat with peas.
> Good corn'd beef, with cabbage boil'd
> Table cloth (with gravy soil'd),
> Spread with pisco-punch so fine,
> Beer, champagne, and first rate wine,
> Turkeys, chickens, turtle soup,
> Roasted plover—quite a troop!
> Onions, craw-fish, pigeons, salad—
> Then the Major's favorite ballad!

Major Warren was described as "a gentleman with a smiling visage, a rotund figure, a disposition like a sunbeam, and a heart as big as the Island of Hawaii".

The building became the Canton Hotel in 1844, and from 1877 to 1898 it was Frederick Horn's Pioneer Steam Candy Manufactory and Bakery.

The Empire Building

41-49 S. Hotel / 1041-1051 Bethel

1950

Designed by Chinese-American architect Yuk Tong Char in 1950 for the Empire Amusement Corp., this 3-story building with 6 stores, 36 offices and modern billiard parlor replaced the Empire Theater built here in 1909.

The theater seated 1,000 people with an entrance on Bethel Street for the 10¢ and 15¢ seats, and an entrance on Hotel Street for the 25¢ gallery seats upstairs. Opening day was Saturday, May 15, 1909.

George W. Houghtailing's Bay Horse Saloon was on the corner from 1855 to 1895.

Bay Horse Saloon.
G. S. HOUGHTAILING, Prop'r.
Cor. Hotel St. and Rose Lane,
HONOLULU, H. I.
The Best of WINES, LIQUORS and CIGARS always on Hand.

It became the Palace Restaurant in 1896 run by Ah Hee & Co. when the government refused to renew the Bay Horse liquor license. It later became the Favorite Grotto Saloon.

Bethel Street

Bethel Street was named for the Seamen's Bethel church at King and Bethel Streets, and initially ran only between Merchant Street and King Street.

It was extended to take over Rose Lane between King and Hotel streets in 1887, then further to Pauahi Street in 1924, and then to Beretania Street in 1927. In the other direction, it was extended to Queen Street in 1931.

Hawaii Theater

1130 Bethel

1922

Proclaimed the "Pride of the Pacific" when it was completed in 1922 for Consolidated Amusements, the Hawaii Theater was designed by Emory & Webb with "hints of Corinthian and Byzantine" architecture, and it was built by the Pacific Engineering Company for close to $500,000.

Construction began on June 10, 1921, and it replaced the Bijou Theater which was previously on the site.

The theater was "Hawaii-designed and Hawaii-built" and seated 1,800 on the main floor and the balcony. It had 2,000 light bulbs connected with 76,000 feet of wire, with marble and tile work by J. Arthur Reed and Frank L. McAfee, sculptured decorations by Julian Rosenstein, and mosaic in the great dome by Gordon Usborne.

The theater had a "heroic-sized" painting 50' long and 20' high above the stage by Lionel Walden titled "The Glorification of the Drama" that was "allegorical to the nth degree... it represents the progress of the race, especially in so far as the finer arts are concerned, from the days of long ago down to this, the twentieth century".

The orchestra pit included a Robert Morgan Unified Orchestral pipe organ with four manuals and 72 stops that took six months to build and was said to be one of the best ever built for theater work.

There was a "honeymoon box" way up in the balcony next to the projection room with an upholstered railing and wicker furniture. "It is more or less removed from the rest of the house, and will prove a boon to honeymooners who, in the past, have been forced to spoon under his hat or her veil while at the theater."

They advertised "30 pretty Chinese girls will usher you to your seat" dressed in "varied costumes of the land of their ancestors". Features included motion pictures, vaudeville, live theater, concerts, and touring acts.

The opening of the theater generated tremendous excitement and the *Honolulu Star-Bulletin* published a 14-page supplement especially for the Hawaii Theater on September 6, 1922.

The Hawaii Theater closed in 1984 and was threatened with demolition. Luckily, a group of concerned citizens formed a non-profit to save the building and raise money for a $32M renovation led by Malcolm Holzman of Hardy Holzman Pfeiffer from New York.

It reopened in 1996, with exterior renovations completed in 2004, including replication of the original 1938 lighted marquee. The League of Historic American Theatres named it an "Outstanding Historic Theatre in America" and the National Trust for Historic Preservation gave it the highest Honor Award.

CHINATOWN GATEWAY PLAZA

1031 Nu'uanu

1990

Designed by Norman Lacayo and completed in 1990, the Chinatown Gateway Plaza is a mixed-use residential-commercial 27-story tower developed by the City of Honolulu containing 200 rental units, approx. 30,000 square feet of commercial space, plus an underground parking garage for 280 cars. The project also includes a landscaped plaza across the street adjacent to the Hawaii Theater.

It is also the home of the Downtown Art Center's extensive gallery, workshop, and exhibition spaces.

On the Hotel and Nu'uanu street sides of the building are 12 textured bronze medallions of the Chinese Zodiac by artist Jill Burkee, installed in 1994. She has studios in New York City, Long Island, and Italy.

The Waverley Block was previously on this corner.

Built for William Mutch by Carl H. Patzig, it initially housed the Ordway & Porter furniture store along with S. Ozaki and The Kash. The Waverley Club met upstairs in Waverley Hall.

THE WAVERLEY BLOCK.

The *Paradise of the Pacific* magazine established its office on the first floor with printing plant on the second floor, in 1905.

While other buildings on Nuʻuanu Street were being demolished in 1970 for a city parking lot, a 21-year-old vagrant started a fire in the Waverley Block that destroyed it and burned 2/3 of the block.

This was also the site of the 2-story coral and wood National House Hotel, built by James Booth in 1847 for the enormous sum of $10,000. It had 7 bedrooms upstairs with a restaurant below. By 1868 it was known as the International Hotel.

Paul Emmert

Its walls were badly cracked in the 1871 earthquake, and during the 1886 fire it was stripped and the veranda pulled down to prevent it catching fire.

This stopped the progress of the fire and saved the buildings on Fort Street, but it damaged the hotel beyond repair.

The site was vacant for 10 years after the 1886 fire and for many years was the location for a popular steam-powered merry-go-round.

CHINATOWN GATEWAY LIONS

1989

Kaohsiung-Honolulu Fellowship

"These two lucky lions symbolize the long-standing friendship and eternal brotherhood between the people of the sister cities of Kaohsiung and Honolulu. The lions are a gift of the City of Kaohsiung to commemorate the 200th anniversary celebration in 1989 of the first Chinese in Hawaii."

Courtesy of Mayor Su Nan Cheng, City of Kaohsiung, Taiwan, Republic of China.

"A School Boy in Hawaii"

2007

Chu Tat-shing, artist

"Chinatown Gateway Park" was renamed to "Dr. Sun Yat-sen Memorial Park" in 2007 and included a statue of Dr. Sun Yat-sen when the first president of the Republic of China and father of modern China was a 13-year-old student at Iolani School.

Chu Tat-shing (朱達誠) is a Chinese sculptor and visual artist from Wuhan, famous for his calligraphy statues, statue of Bruce Lee in Hong Kong, and four statues of Dr. Sun Yat-sen in Hawaii, Wuhan, and Hong Kong.

CHINATOWN

The first Chinese seen in Hawaii were two or three cooks who prepared food for the ship captains in the sandalwood trade in 1789. In China, Hawaii was called 檀香山 (Tánxiāngshān) which translates to "Sandalwood Mountain".

After that initial encounter, the Chinese who came to Hawaii after that were not cooks or laborers – they were ship captains and businessmen. *The Polynesian* published a "Register of Foreigners Residing in Honolulu" on January 9, 1847, and out of the 350 names listed, 12 were obviously Chinese.

The Chinese did not settle exclusively in Chinatown but were mixed in with the general population, and many were married to Hawaiian women. By the 1830's several had already set up shop in Honolulu, including Wong Tai Hoon who owned a store at the ewa/makai corner of Hotel and Nuʻuanu streets.

These early Chinese businessmen were mostly Punti from the Canton (Guangzhou) area while many of the laborers imported later were Hakka from Fukien. Although they had a common written language, the cultures and spoken languages were very different and many subsequently used spoken Hawaiian to communicate.

China was known as the Celestial Empire 天朝 (Tiāncháo), "heavenly dynasty", and the Chinese in Hawaii were often referred to as "Celestials".

On January 3, 1852, the *Thetis* arrived from China with 195 contract laborers – the first ever imported by the government of Hawaii and the first of what would become a tidal wave of immigration. With horrific clan wars in China at the time, many were more than eager to start a new life elsewhere.

Hawaii State Archives

The Chinese men were hard workers, but they did not like the plantation working conditions and most did not renew their contracts. Instead of returning to China many moved to town to become merchants. It has been estimated that 60 percent of the stores in Honolulu were Chinese-owned by 1880.

The rapid influx of laborers that began in the late 1870's required lots of new housing, and wooden apartments and barracks were quickly constructed and packed into existing spaces in Chinatown.

Hawaii State Archives

The first newspaper reference of the name "Chinatown" occurs in 1876, and it was called "Old Chinatown" by 1909.

Chinatown was the working-class area of Honolulu – the main business district was centered around Merchant Street and Fort Street, and the finer residential areas were mauka from Hotel Street.

But the Chinese were not the only foreigners living in Chinatown. The sugar planters also brought in Japanese, Portuguese, Puerto Rican, Korean, Filipino, and even Russian workers.

The first group of Japanese arrived in 1868. They were known as the *gannen-mono* – the "first-year people" since they came to Hawaii in the first year of the reign of Emperor Meiji.

Their travel was fully paid, and their contract called for a salary of $4 per month including room and board for 3 years. But most were craftsmen and not farmers and many returned to Japan, which caused the Japanese government to ban all emigration until King Kalākaua promised better pay, medical care, and a food allowance in 1885.

Instead of only bringing in single men like the planters had done with the Chinese, this time they encouraged wives and families to emigrate to Hawaii, hoping it would result in a more stable workforce. By 1900 there were over 60,000 Japanese in Hawaii – 40% of the total population of the islands.

Japan lifted the ban on emigration from Okinawa in 1900 and by 1920 there were nearly 20,000 Okinawans in Hawaii.

But poor working conditions on the plantations led to protests and confrontations, and the Japanese organized major labor strikes in 1909 and 1920.

And as with the Chinese before, few Japanese stayed on the plantations past their 3-year contracts, preferring instead to move to town and open businesses or start their own farms.

The Federal Immigration Act of 1924 put an end to immigration from Japan, but by that time over 180,000 Japanese had moved to Hawaii.

The first generation were called = *Issei* 一世

Second generation = *Nisei* 二世

Third generation = *Sansei* 三世

Fourth generation = *Yonsei* 四世

Hawaii State Archives

The plantation strikes created a fair amount of anti-Japanese sentiment, but it was nothing like the reaction to the bombing of Pearl Harbor on December 7, 1941. Hundreds of Japanese were arrested, businesses were shut down, and many were sent to the internment camp at Honouliuli on Oahu and to camps on the US mainland.

Many of the Nisei, born in Hawaii as American citizens, worked hard to prove their loyalty in spite of overwhelming wartime suspicions. Initially prevented from serving in the US military, Japanese-Americans were finally accepted and trained as military specialists and soldiers.

The most famous Nisei unit was the 100th Battalion which later became the 442nd Regimental Combat Team that was decorated for their efforts in the war in Europe. President Harry Truman told them, *"You fought not only the enemy, but you fought prejudice and you have won".*

The first Portuguese arrived as sailors on board whaling ships in the mid 1800's.

Concerned about the growing numbers of Chinese being brought into the islands, the government looked to other countries to provide laborers and decided to focus on the Portuguese island territories of Madeira and the Azores.

The bark *Priscilla* brought the first 120 immigrants from Madeira in 1878, and the *Ravenscrag* brought the second contingent of Portuguese in 1879.

There were three luthiers on board the *Ravenscrag* – Manuel Nunes, José do Espírito Santo, and Augusto Dias – and they created Hawaii's most-famous musical instrument – the ukulele.

Adapted from a small Portuguese guitar-like instrument called a *braguinha*, "ukulele" is Hawaiian for "jumping flea", and the name was in common usage by 1888.

Nunes had a shop in Chinatown and claimed credit for inventing the ukulele in 1879.

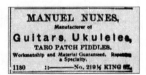

MANUEL NUNES,
Manufacturer of
Guitars, Ukuleles,
TARO PATCH FIDDLES.
Workmanship and Material Guaranteed. Repairing a Specialty.
1180   ::————No. 219½ KING ST.

ᴛʜᴇ ᴄʜɪɴᴀᴛᴏᴡɴ ꜰɪʀᴇꜱ

Chinatown suffered two disastrous fires – in 1886 and 1900. Although much of Chinatown was destroyed, the main business district was spared.

APRIL 18, 1886

Hawaiian Historical Society

By the 1880's, Chinatown was densely packed with mostly 2-story wooden tenements and stores in large blocks with overhanging balconies on both sides of narrow streets, and maybe even a few remaining thatched houses. Many buildings contained cooking fires, kerosene, and other flammable goods, even fireworks.

On April 18, 1886, a fire started in a large Chinese restaurant at the corner of Hotel and Smith streets. From the official report to His Majesty the King:

"The Chinese examined state as their belief that a gambling game or lottery, in which a large number of tickets were used, was in progress. A dispute arose, and the tickets were seized by one of those present and thrust into a fire, which was burning in

the room. A scuffle then ensued, during which the fire was scattered over the floor, and in a moment the room was in a blaze. Some twenty or more Chinamen were seen running out from the upper story when the fire broke out."

The fire spread quickly and caused about $1.5M in damage in Chinatown, burning the businesses and homes of 7,000 Chinese and 350 Hawaiians, and coming very close to burning the whole of Honolulu.

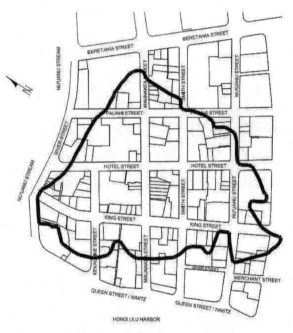

Unable to require everything to be built back in brick or stone, the government created a Fire Limit Line around downtown that required fire-proof construction for all new buildings. This line cut through half of Chinatown, approximately following Maunakea and Smith streets. Outside the line, wooden construction was still allowed. But these wooden structures suffered greatly in 1900.

DECEMBER 31, 1899 TO

JANUARY 20, 1900

There was not just one Chinatown fire in 1900 – there were 9 of them. They started on December 31, 1899, and continued to the big out-of-control fire on January 20, 1900.

All of the fires were started by the Honolulu Fire Department under the direction of the Board of Health.

Although rats around the harbor had been mysteriously dying in large numbers in late 1899, no one was alarmed until a 22-year-old bookkeeper named You Chong was diagnosed with bubonic plague on December 11, 1899, dying the next day of the horrific disease. Others soon followed.

The Board of Health essentially took over the government, cordoned off Chinatown with a wooden fence, and began a series of fumigations and controlled burns in an attempt to stop the spread of plague.

Where outbreaks of plague had occurred, buildings of brick or stone were closed up and fumigated, but wooden structures could not be made airtight so they were ordered to be burned. And sometimes not just single buildings but entire blocks were condemned and reduced to ashes.

The standard procedure was to select a day with calm winds, place fire-fighting equipment at strategic locations around the perimeter, and then start the fire on the downwind side and let it slowly burn against the wind while maintaining steady flows of water on adjacent structures intended to be spared.

Most of the controlled burns were in Chinatown, but they also occurred in other places throughout the city where plague had been found.

Residents were given short notice to pile their belongings in the street, to be burned or sent for fumigation, and they were then forcibly evacuated while their residences and businesses were put to the torch.

There were 9 separate burns in Chinatown, from single buildings to entire blocks, starting with a few buildings on the waikiki side of Nuʻuanu Street at Pauahi Street on December 31, 1899.

On January 20, the fire department was burning infected buildings behind Kaumakapili Church when the wind suddenly changed direction and began to blow with great force. They tried valiantly to keep sparks away from the church but burning embers made it to one of the steeples and it caught fire out of reach of their hoses.

The steeple burned like a giant sparkler with the strong wind sending flaming cinders all across Chinatown. People tried in vain to put out fires on their buildings and rooftops, but they were no match for the wind and the sparks and the rapidly spreading fire. By the end of the day over 29 acres of houses and buildings had been burned and half of Chinatown had been completely destroyed.

Hawaii State Archives

Honolulu's Royal Mile

EXTENTS OF THE 1900 FIRES

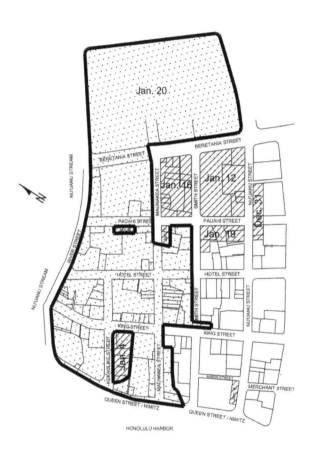

Nuʻuanu Street

Nuʻuanu translates to "cool cliff", a reference to it extending up the Nuʻuanu Valley to the Pali.

This was one of the most important streets in town for many years, since it was the only one that connected directly to the wharfs at the harbor.

Looking mauka from Hotel Street, c.1885

Looking mauka from Hotel Street, c.1902

Looking makai from Hotel Street, c.1880

Hotel Street, looking waikiki from Nuʻuanu Street

Hotel Street, looking ewa from Nuʻuanu Street

𝔓erry 𝔅lock

1101-1111 Nuʻuanu, 2-8 S. Hotel
1888

Built on the site of a large coral stone store from 1867, this classic Eastlake Victorian building was designed by Isaac A. Palmer and built by E.B. Thomas in 1888 for $15,952.

It was built for Anna Dos Anjos Henriques from the island of Fayal in the Azores. She was the widow of former Portuguese consul Jacinto Pereira, also known as Jason Perry.

If you look closely you can see the Portuguese coat of arms incorporated into the keystones of the first-floor windows and doorways.

The first businesses here were the Yokohama Bazaar and M. Chiya & Company.

Bill Lederer's Bar was here from 1940 to 1985. It was a "hard-drinking saloon without fancy frills" that was often visited by Muhammed Ali as well as a 320-pound bosun's mate who would ride his Harley-Davidson motorcycle into the bar, down a drink, and then ride out.

Edgar William Leeteg was also a frequent customer who often paid his bar tab with paintings. Called "the Remington of the South Seas" by James Michener, Leeteg was also known as the "Father of Velvet Paintings" and was famous for images of sensuous Tahitian women that sold for as much as $20,000. His estate in Tahiti was called "Villa Velour".

From 1988 to 2000 the Chinatown police station was located here, the joke at the time being that "there were nearly as many cops in the place as when it was a bar".

THE COSMOPOLITAN SALOON

1058 Nu'uanu, 11 N. Hotel
1886

This was the first brick building completed after the disastrous 1886 fire. It was built "in six weeks and a day" by George Lucas from County Clare, Ireland, for George Freeth and Walter Peacock. They were the largest saloon owners and wholesale liquor dealers of their day.

Known as the Cosmopolitan Saloon, the interior was "wainscoted in redwood with black walnut graining, and the bar was topped with solid black walnut".

The Cosmopolitan Restaurant/Hotel/Saloon initially opened on this site in 1881 with proprietor Peter Acosta, formerly the Chief Steward of the steamer *Likelike*.

The dinner menu included crab salad "with all the etceteras", plus "roast goose stuffed with sage and onions and served with apple sauce". Favorite beers were Pabst Milwaukee and Buffalo Beer.

The Cosmopolitan Saloon was on this corner for 22 years from 1881 to 1903. It was renamed "The California" and operated by State Representative Henry C. Vida but was foreclosed in 1905 by the Sheriff for not paying the liquor license fee. Everything was sold at public auction including a 22-foot oak bar with mahogany top and a 19-foot oak bar with large beveled mirrors.

From 1914 to 1952 this was the New York Shoe Store owned by Choy Hoy An. He was a native of Seongchak village in South China and had come to Honolulu as a boy. His wife, Mrs. Choy Chang See, ran the business for 20 years after his death in 1932.

In 1952 she sold the business to James V. Kunst from Prague, Czechoslovakia, who renamed it the "Ka-ma-aina Shoe Store". He retained many of the former employees, some of whom had worked in the New York Store for 25 years.

 In the 1830's this was the site of an adobe building that was a Chinese store owned by Wong Tyhoon. It was the second Chinese store in Honolulu, and he sold dry goods, groceries, wines, spirits, and had rooms and opium dens in back for fellow Chinese. Tyhoon also had stores in Koloa and Lahaina plus interests in sugar and shipping.

Encore Saloon

1102-1112 Nuʻuanu, 2-20 N. Hotel
1887

After the April 1886 Chinatown fire destroyed the 2-story wooden building on this corner, Joseph Mendonça hired George Lucas to build this building for $9,554 with 8 storefronts with rooms up above. Most of the first businesses were Chinese, mostly selling general merchandise.

During restoration of the building in the 1980's they reportedly found a "Shanghai compartment" between the floor and the ceiling with a trap door, the idea being that drugged/drunk sailors would be kidnapped and held here until ship captains paid to have them sent to ships bound for places like Shanghai. There is nothing in the historical record to confirm this, and the days of sail were drawing to a close by the late 1880's, but it certainly might have been used for hiding opium or smuggling.

ENCORE SALOON

Choice Wines, Liquors and Cigars.
RYAN & DEMENT.
Northwest corner Hotel and Nuuanu
Streets.

Paddy Ryan and Charles Dement opened the Encore Saloon at this corner in 1901. Paddy, the bartender, was known for the catchphrase "What are you going to take?"

Hawaii State Archives

You can see how narrow Nuʻuanu Street was in the 1800's before all the buildings were either moved or torn down and rebuilt to allow for the street width we see today.

Louis Warren bought the business in 1907 and moved it diagonally across the street in 1908.

This rare photograph was taken about 1880 and shows the 2-story wooden building that was on this site before the 1886 fire.

I.W. Taber

It housed a dry goods store on the corner as well as a barber shop as evidenced by the striped pole.

Paiko Block / Lai Fong Building

1118-1120 Nuʻuanu
1880

Next to the Encore Saloon Building is the second-oldest building in Chinatown and one of the few survivors of the 1886 Chinatown fire – but only just barely. It was built in 1880 by S.D. Burrows for Portuguese immigrant Manuel Paiko, and it was one of the first substantial brick buildings in Chinatown.

The first stores to move into the new Paiko Block were the Hollister Drug Store on the left and the Goo Kim dry goods store on the right.

Its construction was severely tested on April 18, 1886, when it became "a great burning cauldron within, the flames bursting out around the iron shutters". Firemen attempted to put out the fire in the building but "the shutters which kept the fire in also kept the water out". These same iron shutters are still visible on both sides of the building today.

The good news was this brick building stopped the fire from spreading across Nuʻuanu Street toward downtown.

The building looked very different when it was first built in 1880. Although made of brick, the front was stuccoed and scored to look like stone blocks.

Lai Fong was the daughter of a village chief in Canton (Guanghzou), China, and was a "picture bride" who was chosen by the parents of her future husband, Edward Au, who had fought with Dr. Sun Yat-sen in the 1911 Chinese Revolutionary War. They moved to Hawaii in 1913.

She opened her first store in 1934, moved here in 1947.

Lai Fong made Chinese gowns and sold silk cloth, clothing, furniture, jewelry, and screens.

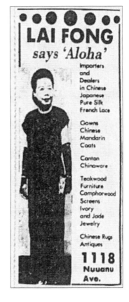

LAI FONG
says 'Aloha'

Importers
and
Dealers
in Chinese
Japanese
Pure Silk
French Lace

Gowns
Chinese
Mandarin
Coats

Canton
Chinaware

Teakwood
Furniture
Camphorwood
Screens
Ivory
and Jade
Jewelry

Chinese Rugs
Antiques

1118
Nuuanu
Ave.

Smith's Union Bar

15-19 N. Hotel
c.1904

Claiming to be Honolulu's oldest bar, Smith's Union Bar is a favorite watering hole for merchant seamen and survivors of the USS Arizona.

Built around 1904, there was a shooting gallery in this building until about 1927. Targets were 40' away and a bell rang when a bullseye was hit.

It was owned by T.H. Thone, described as "a big husky fellow" who obviously enjoyed shooting – on April 29, 1901, he fired four shots at his quarrelsome father-in-law.

In 1934 this was Joe Holley's Café, and it has been Smith's Union Bar since 1939.

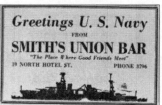

CLUB HUBBA HUBBA

21-25 N. Hotel
1886

This building was built in 1886 by George Lucas for Supreme Court Judge Richard Bickerton.

It initially housed the S. Kojima store, then the Green Front Café, and then Buck's Mickey Mouse café which advertised being the home of "Bunny Ranch triple decker sandwiches".

The most famous business in this building started off as a sandwich shop and quickly devolved into a showplace – from live cowboy hillbilly music to "strippers galore".

Café Hubba Hubba opened in 1946, turning into Club Hubba Hubba in 1954.

Although the phrase "hubba hubba" had been in circulation for a few years, it was made popular by American servicemen and Bob Hope during World War II, and also by the singing of Perry Como and Martha Stewart in the 1945 movie *Doll Face*.

The café had featured live cowboy bands, but the club was all about burlesque. There were 4 evening shows with a "femcee", with dancing to live music in between.

The interior was red and black with a large lighted Plexiglas catwalk. A dancer once asked the night manager for a glass of water and was told, "get a customer to buy it for you".

In 1962 one of the exotic dancers shot and killed her former cop ex-husband at the club. The bar stayed open and everyone continued drinking.

Many of the dancers lived upstairs in tiny rooms, and in its later days the club was described as "grossly accented with the miasma of stale beer, cigarette smoke, roach spray, cheap perfume, and Pine-Sol".

The club finally closed in 1996 and the building was restored in 2010. Special approval was granted to restore the original neon sign made by Robert "Bozo" Shigemura.

Do you think Judge Bickerton would have approved of dancer Tanya Tata's "Biggest Chest in the Midwest" at 60KK-24-36?

℞ISQUE ℞HEATRE / ℞UFFUM'S ℞ALL

32-36 N. Hotel
c.1902

This is the site of Buffum's Hall, built by Dr. A.C. Buffum in 1870. It was the scene of lectures, prestidigitation, escamotage, recitations, tableaux, minstrel shows, masquerade balls, pantomimes, and tricks of legerdemain featuring such luminaries as Madame Cora de Lamond, Madame Carandini, and Professor Louis Hazelmayer.

Sanford Dole read Irving's *Rip Van Winkle* here (described as "rather lengthy and tedious"), and Hawaiian royalty were regularly in attendance.

Dr. Buffum returned to California in 1871 and the building was leased on off-nights for the Honolulu Skating Rink. Queen Emma attended opening night on July 22, 1871, which featured a Grand March, Plain Quadrille, Lancers, Queen's Quadrille, and Virginia Reel – *all danced on skates!*

The hall was destroyed in the 1886 fire and the building here today was built about 1902.

It housed the Trade Winds Café from 1941 to 1961, advertising "the Jiviest Jazz in Town", and later the Show Bar.

It became the Risque Theater in 1969, specializing in sexually oriented adult films and magazines, with the Risque II Theater upstairs, the first gay adult theater in downtown Honolulu.

The Risque Theatre was here for over 20 years.

Honolulu's Royal Mile

THE SWING CLUB

35-43-49 N. Hotel
1886

Consisting of three different storefronts, this building was built in 1886 by "Chinese builders".

Originally housing Chinese and Japanese stores, by the 1940's it was full of amusement centers and bars catering to the massive influx of military personnel to Hawaii during World War II.

These amusement centers typically featured a wide range of games of skill and of chance, billiard tables, barber shops, cafés, soda fountains, and sometimes shooting galleries, all attended to by attractive female hostesses.

Many also featured photo booths where a sailor could pay to have his picture taken with a hula girl. These were hugely popular souvenir items, and sometimes got a little carried away.

At Victory Amusement here in 1944, "hula poser" Mrs. Isabella Guzman Torres and the photographer were arrested for "posing in an indecent manner" and fined $50. It had attracted 50 sailors so it must have been pretty racy!

The Swing Club opened on the left side in 1955, billed as "the only place where the happenings are always happening".

The guest musicians and house band transitioned to go-go girls in cages by the mid-1960's. One of the more unusual acts was Little Johnny Shaw – "36-inches Tall 'n Full of Soul, the James Brown of the Dwarf Set".

In 1971 the Swing Club became an X-rated live sex nightclub with X-rated movies upstairs. That same year 26-year-old future porn star John Holmes was arrested here for lewd acts on stage.

The middle storefront was briefly the Sai Fu Chop Sui House in the 1920's, and the downtown location of P.Y. Chong's famous Waikiki restaurant Lau Yee Chai in the 1930's. It became the Anchor Club in 1955 featuring country and hillbilly music, and then the Anchor Bar with topless dancers by the mid-1970's.

The Kwong Hang Chan & Company general merchandise store was originally on the corner, and then the G. Wong Sun & Company grocery store. In 1949 it became John Welch's Porthole, "The Home of Western and Hill-Billy Entertainment", and then Tammy's Lounge in 1965 with topless go-go dancers.

40 N. HOTEL

1892

A rather unassuming building today, it was initially a 2-stsory building built in 1892, but everything changed when the front façade collapsed in 1980.

From 1910 until 1932 it housed some pretty serious revolutionary activity – it was the office of the Chee Yow Shin Bo, known as the Liberty News Chinese newspaper, with offices of the Oahu Kuomintang on the second floor.

In 1910, before he overthrew the Qing Dynasty and became the first president of the Chinese Republic, Dr. Sun Yat-sen often came to work here.

50 N. HOTEL

50 N. Hotel
1897, 1901, 1980 remodel

The 1886 fire started here. At the time, Smith's Lane was just a narrow little pathway located on the far side of present-day Smith Street, and there was a huge 2-story 35' x 60' wooden Chinese restaurant where the street is today.

On April 18, 1886, a dispute upstairs over a gambling game resulted in paper tickets being thrown into a fire, with the resultant scuffle spreading the fire throughout the room, and within a few hours engulfing most of Chinatown.

The fire spread in all directions from this corner and burned over 21 acres. Sailors from ships in harbor helped fight the fire, as did future king David Kalākaua.

Hawaii State Archives

Honolulu's Royal Mile

$SMITH$ $STREET$

Smith Street was originally a crooked little path called Smith's Lane between Beretania and Hotel streets. It was widened and extended after the disastrous 1886 Chinatown fire.

Reverend Lowell Smith was born in Heath, Massachusetts in 1802 and became an ordained minister. He came to Hawaii in 1832 aboard the ship *Mentor* after a voyage of 161 days.

Initially stationed at Molokai, in 1836 he became the first superintendent of Kawaiahaʻo School and for thirty years was the pastor of Kaumakapili Church.

Smith lived on the ewa side of the street next to a schoolhouse he built in 1837. The first church services for Kaumakapili Church ("the native church") were held in that schoolhouse before the parishioners built a huge adobe and thatch church building on the other side of Beretania Street in 1839.

KAUMAKAPILI CHURCH
(SITE)

Mauka side of Beretania at Smith

Hawaii State Archives

If you look mauka on Smith Street toward Beretania Street, just past the far end of Smith you will see the site of two Kaumakapili Churches.

Known as the Native's Church, it started off as a massive 60' x 125' adobe building with thatch roof built by the parishioners and dedicated in 1839.

The old adobe church was torn down in 1881 to make way for a grand new structure with twin steeples suggested by King Kalākaua who said, "a man has two arms, two eyes, two ears, two legs, therefore a church ought to have two steeples".

The church was designed by Charles J. Wall and construction started in 1881. The first tower was completed in 1884, the second in 1885, and the building was officially dedicated on Sunday, June 10, 1888.

It would have been visible today at the head of Smith Street except for one fateful day in 1900.

On January 20, 1900, in the midst of the plague, the fire department was burning some small buildings near the back of the church when the wind suddenly shifted and increased in intensity.

Although the firemen valiantly tried to protect the church, sparks flew to one of the steeples, out of reach, and it subsequently caught fire and burned like a giant sparkler showering flaming embers all across Chinatown.

The fire burned 29 acres of Chinatown and left the church a smoldering ruin. It was sold two years later to be hauled away by contractor Pang Chong.

Hawaii State Archives

Joseph P. Mendonça Building

54-74 N. Hotel, 1112-1116 Smith, 1113 Maunakea
1901

This is the largest historical building in Chinatown, built in 1901 after the 1900 fire destroyed everything on the block.

It was designed by architect Oliver Traphagen who submitted three different designs for consideration to owner Joseph P. Mendonça.

The building was restored in 1978 by Bob Gerell and Pete Smith, and their huge leap of faith sparked a much-needed wave of historic preservation throughout Chinatown, with Gerell and Smith restoring many buildings themselves.

Not even open one year yet, the Mendonça Building experienced its first gambling raid on June 18,1902 – the largest one to that date in the history of the Honolulu Police Department, with 96 Chinese arrested in an upstairs room at 11:30 am on the Maunakea side.

Knowing they were being watched by the gambler's lookouts, Deputy High Sheriff Chillingworth and his men stayed calm in the street while Detective David Kaapa led a posse of Native Hawaiians who used a ladder and crowbars to break through a window and four barricaded doors.

Inside they found five tables for pai gow, fan tan and other gambling games. The four dealers managed to escape through a trap door in the roof with two tins and two sacks of money.

Born in the Azores in 1847, Joseph Paul Mendonça came to Hawaii as a whaling ship galley hand and first worked for his uncle Jason Perry. He acquired lots of land particularly in Chinatown, created the Kaneohe Ranch, and was active in the overthrow of the Hawaiian monarchy in 1893.

Before the 1900 fire there were five 2-story wooden buildings on this site, with several butchers, doctors, barbers, restaurants, general merchandise stores, and a cake bakery. There was a fancy second-floor gallery on the ewa/makai corner that was possibly an upstairs dining area for a restaurant.

1913 Mendonca Building

51-55 N. Hotel, 1042 Smith

1913

Sometimes called the Mini Mendonça Building, this building was designed by Harry L. Kerr and built by George M. Yamada in 1913.

Before the 1900 fire it was the site of a 2-story wooden building housing a barber shop on the corner, another barber shop next door, and a fruit store that replaced an earlier 2-story wooden drug store that burned in the 1886 fire.

The concrete building here today has a footprint of only 980 square feet and according to the March 22, 1913, building permit announcement it cost $6,700.

For 32 years it was the home of Sing Kee Jewelry, but then became the Mini Theatre and later the Bijou Theatre showing pornographic films.

Two of the leading lights of Chinatown historic preservation once officed upstairs – architects Spencer Leineweber and Glenn Mason.

By the mid 1990's this area was overrun with drug dealers and users, "the worst corner in Chinatown", and the building was taken in a drug forfeiture.

Maunakea Street

Dating back before there were any Chinese in what is now called Chinatown, Maunakea Street was a major commercial street along with Hotel and King streets.

The name translates to "White Mountain", and historically was spelled either as "Mauna Kea" or "Maunakea".

It was perhaps named after the largest mountain in the Hawaiian Islands – the Mauna Kea volcano on the Island of Hawaii.

WO FAT RESTAURANT

111 N. Hotel

1938

This building is without a doubt the spiritual and cultural center of Chinatown. And no, it's not named for the primary villain in the *Hawaii 5-0* TV series – the TV name comes from this restaurant, Wo Fat, which translates to "Peace and Prosperity".

Famous for its Chinese-style architecture and commanding presence at the corner of Hotel and Maunakea, the Wo Fat Chop Sui House was one of the premier Chinese restaurants in Honolulu.

Designed by Yuk Tong Char in 1938, the Wo Fat Restaurant was a legendary dining spot for over 50 years. It had elaborately painted designs on the ceiling and walls, and could seat 1,000 people.

A liquor store and bar were on the first floor, the restaurant on the second floor. The octagonal Dragon Room in the corner Pagoda and the rooftop pavilion could be reserved for private parties.

Opening day to much fanfare and fireworks was March 10, 1938.

The elaborate painting on the walls, beams and ceiling was by Tadao Takeuchi in the colors of a building from Nanjing, learned from consulting with the Chinese art records at the Honolulu Academy of Arts.

Many rich and famous have dined here over the years including Frank Sinatra and Jackie Kennedy plus TV producer Leonard Freeman who created the original *Hawaii 5-0* TV series in 1968.

According to company lore, the Wo Fat restaurant began in Chinatown in 1881. The first newspaper mention of Wo Fat's "Chinese lunch room" in this location is on December 16, 1896. On February 1, 1897, Wat Ging and seven other Chinese formed the baking, restaurant, and candy business "Wo Fat and Nee Chong".

After the new Lum Yip Kee building went up next door in 1936, Wo Fat announced in 1937 that they would also be demolishing their old wooden building for a new 3-story concrete structure that would occupy the whole corner.

The current Wo Fat building was built on the site of a large wooden Wo Fat restaurant building plus the site of a 2-story coral building known as Liberty Hall.

NEW HOTEL
LIBERTY HALL.

The above House has recently been opened as a first class Hotel. No expense has been spared in fitting it with every modern convenience for comfort and elegance. The Bar will always be supplied with the best of Wines, Liquors and Cigars; and the proprietor hopes by strict attention to the wants of his customers, to merit a share of the public patronage.

JAMES DAWSON.

Honolulu, Sept. 7, 1850.   17 1y.

Hawaii State Archives

This c.1860's photograph shows the back side of Liberty Hall, located on Maunakea Street where the makai end of the Wo Fat Building is today. It opened in 1850 and was one of the most popular drinking establishments and dancing halls in Honolulu.

Kamehameha V and his cabinet were often there, dancing to mazurkas, quadrilles, reels, and lancers with fiddler and dancing master James Old accompanied by piano.

"You asked me about the girls who danced with the boys then... they were excellent dancers and (let me whisper) they were rather good-natured."

The proprietor, James Dawson, also owned several ships involved in the whaling trade – the sloop *Wave* and the schooners *Kinoole*, *Ortolan*, and *Emeline*.

Liberty Hall was closed in 1867 for "selling liquor to natives" and the building was damaged by a big earthquake on February 19,1871. It was briefly a temperance coffee salon & billiard room in 1871 operated by Louis Kahlbaum.

The building was destroyed in the 1886 fire.

In 2017 the Wo Fat building was purchased for $4M with plans to spend another $6M to build dining and retail on the first floor and to convert the upper floors into a 23-room boutique hotel, combining historic preservation with adaptive re-use.

Lum Yip Kee Building

119-131 N. Hotel

1937

Believe it or not, a business in this building was the inspiration for a National Book Award winner voted one of the best novels of the 20th century. The book was subsequently made into a movie that received 13 Academy Award nominations and won 8 Oscars, and the story was also turned into a musical at the Shaftesbury Theatre in London.

This Lum Yip Kee Building was designed by George Hogan of Cain & Awana in 1937 for wealthy Chinese businessman Lum Yip Kee – "The Poi King".

The building's main claim to fame was a business on the second floor run by Dorothy MacCready and Ruth Davis from 1937 to 1944, known as the New Senator Hotel.

It was the largest brothel in Chinatown and employed 15 women, most of whom were imported from the US Mainland.

Sailors would often be lined up around the block for the chance to spend $3 for 3 minutes.

The New Senator Hotel was a favorite haunt of author James Jones who wrote the 1951 best-seller *From Here to Eternity* based on his experiences here.

Hawaiian Historical Society

The book was made into an Academy Award winning movie in 1953 that starred Burt Lancaster, Montgomery Clift, Deborah Kerr, Frank Sinatra, Donna Reed, and Ernest Borgnine.

In the book and in the movie, the name was cleverly changed to the "New Congress Hotel".

Maunakea Marketplace

1989

Designed by architect James K. Sugawa in a public-private partnership between the city and Pauahi Associates (Bob Gerell/Smith & Associates and Mouse Builders Inc.), the $4.6M Maunakea Marketplace is on 46,000 SF of city-owned property in the heart of Chinatown, completed in 1989.

"A few years from now, Chinatown will be one of this state's prime neighborhoods, we believe it will be one of the top tourist attractions, as well as a safe, exciting place to visit for our residents."

Mayor Frank F. Fasi

GLADE SHOW CLUB (SITE)

152-156 N. Hotel

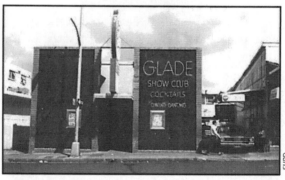

This is the site of the infamous Glade Show Club that featured live music and floor shows with female impersonators from 1964 to 1980. Their advertising slogan was "Boys Will Be Girls".

The master of ceremonies was Liko Johnson – 6 feet tall and 266 pounds with "pancake makeup, a knee-length muumuu, falsies, fake eyelashes, gobs of purple-black eye shadow, a woman's wig and a huge orchid over his left ear".

The most famous and flamboyant entertainer was Henry Kelso Daniel, better known by his stage name of Prince Hanalei. Billed as "The World's Only Male Exotic Dancer", his "twirling torchlight tush" was legendary exotica and consisted of spinning flaming butt tassels.

The Glade was one of nine places in Honolulu that were officially off-limits to servicemen, but of course that didn't stop them from coming in to gawk at the cross-dressers and transexuals and experience a stage show like they would never see back home.

Many of the "queens" (as they called themselves) had a birth name, a street name, and a stage name, and were required by law to wear a large red button in public that said "I Am A Boy".

LUNG DOO BUILDING

159 N. Hotel, 1040 Kekaulike
1965

美國夏威夷隆都從善會

This delightful little building is one of the few Chinese-looking buildings in Chinatown, with its large round red door and distinctive pagoda on top. It was designed by Chinese-American architect James C.M. Young, and it was finished in time for the 75th anniversary of the Lung Doo Benevolent Society in 1965.

Lung Doo is a complex of 56 villages in the city of Zhongshan, southeast of Guangzhou, and the society was founded to provide services and support for Chinese immigrants coming from the areas where the Lung Doo dialect was spoken.

In addition to mutual assistance and protection the society also does charitable work and supports youth education with annual scholarships to Chinese language schools as well as the University of Hawaii.

Winston Hale

158-190 N. Hotel
1965, remodeled 1981

This building was designed by Lemmon Freeth Haines & Jones and built by Town Construction in 1965 on the site of the infamous Winston Block apartments built in 1903 by E.C. Winston.

Rooms in the old Winston Block rented for $2 a month and its residents "figured largely in local criminal history".

Notable activities at the Winston included fighting, gambling, arson, drunkenness, beatings, infidelity, profanity, lewdness, brick-throwing, stabbing, murder, burglary, and Peeping Toms.

Honolulu Police officer Chang Ah Ping, better known as Chang Apana, was a frequent visitor to the Winston Block. His exploits and arrests were legendary, and often involved a bullwhip he still carried from his days working as a paniolo cowboy.

Mystery novelist Earl Derr Biggers heard about Chang Apana in 1925 while writing *The House Without a Key* and promptly inserted a new character into the book based on the Honolulu detective. The character's name? Charlie Chan.

Biggers featured Charlie Chan in 5 more books and the character was featured in nearly 50 films. Chang Apana enjoyed the movies and was often called "Charlie Chan" and asked to sign autographs.

Legendary boxing promoter Sam Ichinose ran Sad Sam's bar at the corner of the Winston Block from 1941 to 1957. Known for his somber expression and incredible energy, Samuel Masuo Ichinose was known as "Mr. Boxing" for over 50 years and staged more than 425 fights in Hawaii, Tokyo, Indonesia, and Europe.

Hawaii State Archives

The City bought the property in 1981 and remodeled it to the way it looks today, claiming at the time that it "was not listed on the State Registry of Historic Places nor is it of any historic or architectural value".

RIVER STREET NU'UANU STREAM

River Street parallels Nu'uanu Stream and was created in 1896 after the re-alignment and channelization of Nu'uanu Stream with stone walls.

Hawaii State Archives

The first Hotel Street bridge was for streetcars only, and was a 108'-long riveted steel truss installed in 1901 by the Honolulu Rapid Transit & Land Co.

Oahu Railway & Land Depot

1925

Hawaii State Archives

The Oahu Railway & Land Company was a narrow-gauge railway and land development company created in 1889 by Benjamin Dillingham.

The first line opened between Honolulu and Aiea on November 16, 1889, with free rides to over 4,000 passengers. The railroad also hauled freight, equipment, mail, and sugar cane workers.

Hawaii State Archives

The current depot replaced the previous wooden building from 1889 which had been enlarged and expanded over the years.

Bertram Goodhue proposed a new design in 1921, but they ended up hiring local architect Guy Rothwell instead. The new depot was completed in 1925.

After many successful years, particularly during World War II, the postwar era along with a tsunami and a sugar strike took its toll, and the last train ran on December 31, 1947.

Today, the Hawaiian Railway Society runs excursion trains on a portion of the track in Kapolei and they also maintain Benjamin Dillingham's private coach.

The depot building is now owned by the State.

ʻAʻALA PARK

Once a thriving working-class community of Chinese, Japanese and Filipino workers, the Aala Triangle neighborhood has been flooded, burned, and deliberately demolished.

Today it is an open park, 6.69 acres in size, extending from Palama Junction where King and Beretania streets meet to Nuʻuanu Stream.

This was initially a low-lying area at the mouth of Nuʻuanu Stream, and although prone to flooding and containing stagnant ponds, it filled up with 2-story wooden buildings to accommodate the influx of Chinese and Japanese immigrants in the late 1800's.

Between 1896 and 1898 the city conducted a large-scale dredging project that straightened Nuʻuanu Stream between stone-lined walls, with much of the dredged materials going to fill in "unsanitary" pools on both sides of the stream.

When bubonic plague struck Honolulu in late 1899, wooden buildings and entire blocks and districts were burned by the Board of Health to try to stop the spread of the disease. The Aala triangle area was burned on January 25, 1900.

AALA DISTRICT IN ASHES

EYESORE TO HONOLULU BURNED THIS MORNING.

Fire Swept From King Street to the Knoll Above Chinese Theaters—Tai Kee's Place Investigated.

The long row of buildings on King street near the Oahu railway depot is in ashes. Included in the burned district are the Bay View hotel, several stores, a restaurant and all the houses back to the junction of Aala lane with Aala road. The old Chinese theater was burned. In fact the whole district was swept, leaving only a charred expanse of valuable land and a great stagnant pool to tell the story. The latter will be filled as soon as possible.

Numbers 2 and 4 engines, assisted by Number 1 hose cart and crew, did the business. The engines went down at 9 o'clock this morning and began the fire at about 10:20. At noon the job was practically complete.

The Hawaiian Star, January 25, 1900

As soon as the embers died down, the city decided to "convert Aala park from a barren waste composed of harbor dredgings into a resort of beauty".

Aala Park. Honolulu.

The park was located adjacent to Nuuanu Stream, while the area between the train station and Palama Junction filled up with commercial and residential buildings along King and Beretania streets.

Hawaii State Archives

Hawaii State Archives

Aala Park became a favorite baseball ground, and it had a bandstand designed by HL Kerr and the first public toilet in Honolulu.

The neighborhood fell into decline after the railroad left in 1947 and the depot was turned into a bus station. Many left due to the allure of the suburbs.

Wholesale destruction occurred once again with Aala Triangle Project No. Hawaii R-3 of the Honolulu Redevelopment Authority, in conjunction with the Urban Renewal Administration, United States Housing and Home Finance Agency in 1968.

The demolition of Aala was poignantly captured in the 26:50-minute film *Aala: A Visual Poem about the Living and Dying of a Community*, by Stephen Bartlett, Kenneth Bushnell, and Francis Haar.

The entire film is online, courtesy of the University of Hawaii at Manoa Library, and can also be viewed at this link:

<u>1107_aala | University of Hawaii at Manoa Library</u>

Later renamed "Aala International Park", the intention was to host a variety of multi-ethnic festivities and events, but that never materialized. But a skate park was installed in 1978 that is still in use today, and a dog park has been recently added.

Unfortunately, Aala Park has been plagued for years with vagrants, crime, and homeless encampments.

The Trust for Public Land is currently working to improve the park as part of its Parks for People program. Artists have recently painted murals on the restroom, skate park, basketball court, planter boxes, and benches. With luck, Aala Park will once again become an inviting urban oasis.

Sources

Hawaii State Archives

Hawaiian Historical Society

Newspapers.com

University of Hawaii at Manoa Library
Digital Image Collections

Gary R. Coover

A Honolulu resident since 2013, Gary has been researching historic properties and neighborhoods throughout the United States for the past 30 years.

He is the author of the *Pocket Walking Tour of Honolulu's Chinatown, Pocket Walking Tour of Old Downtown Honolulu, Honolulu Chinatown: 200 Years of Red Lanterns & Red Lights, Downtown Honolulu's Lost Buildings and Forgotten Architects, Honolulu 1854: The Drawings of Paul Emmert,* and the annotator of *A Tour of Honolulu in the Early 1840's.*

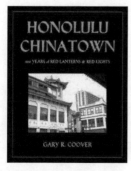

Honolulu's Royal Mile

ᴀʟᴘʜᴀʙᴇᴛɪᴄᴀʟ ɪɴᴅᴇx

Made in the USA
Columbia, SC
10 September 2024